T0025258

Selected Duets

for FLUTE

Published in Two Volumes:

VOLUME I (Easy-Medium)

• VOLUME II (Advanced)

Compiled and Edited

by H. VOXMAN

RUBANK®

HAL•LEONARD®
CORPORATION

7777 W. BLUEMOUND RD. P.O. BOX 13819 MILWAUKEE, WI 53213

PREFACE

Duet playing affords the student the most intimate form of ensemble experience. The problems of technique, tone quality, intonation, and ensemble balance are brought into the sharpest relief. Careful attention must be given to style as indicated by the printed page and as demanded by the intangibles of good taste.

The duets from the eighteenth century, by Loeillet, Telemann, Geminiani, W. F. Bach, and others, present many problems in the interpretation of the ornaments. In general, trills written before the year 1800, and probably many thereafter, should begin with the note above the principal note. For a more detailed treatment of the embellishments used in this publication the student is referred to the Harvard Dictionary of Music and the Grove's Dictionary of Music and Musicians (fifth edition).

The author wishes to express his gratitude to the library of the *British Museum* (London) for the use of collections of flute music found in its music division.

H. Voxman

●

CONTENTS

●

Allegro and Menuett

BEETHOVEN

Duetto No. VI, Op. 101
Based on Quartet, Op. 17, No. 6

HAYDN

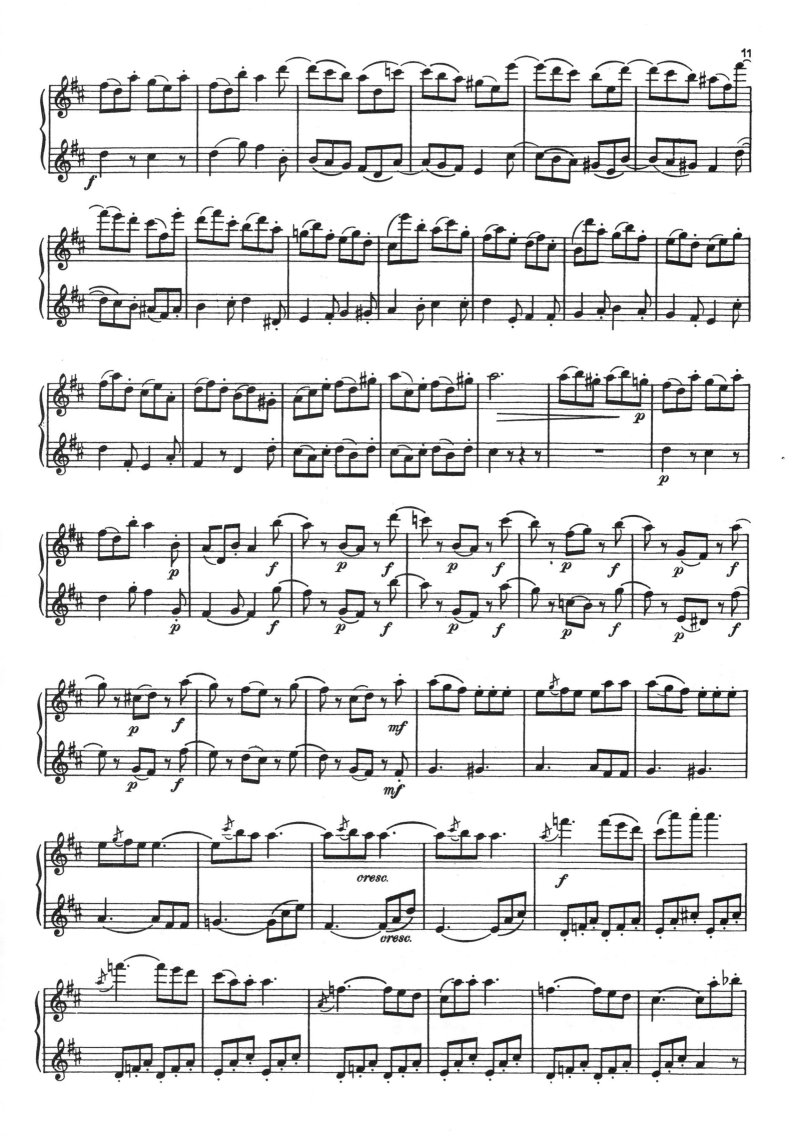

* Play same rhythm as in lower part, i.e., two quarter notes.

14

Allegro

ECHO

HAYDN

Menuetto

TRIO

(After D.C. segue Presto)

Fine

Presto

Seven Duets
Selected from the Works of
W. F. Bach, Devienne, Furstenau, Geminiani, Handel, H. Köhler, and Telemann

FURSTENAU

SONATINE No. V, FROM Op. 96

H. KÖHLER

Allegro

SONATA No. 2

TELEMANN

The second player begins each section when the first player has reached the sign (𝄋).

The second player finishes each section at the first fermata (𝄐), which should not be observed by the first player.

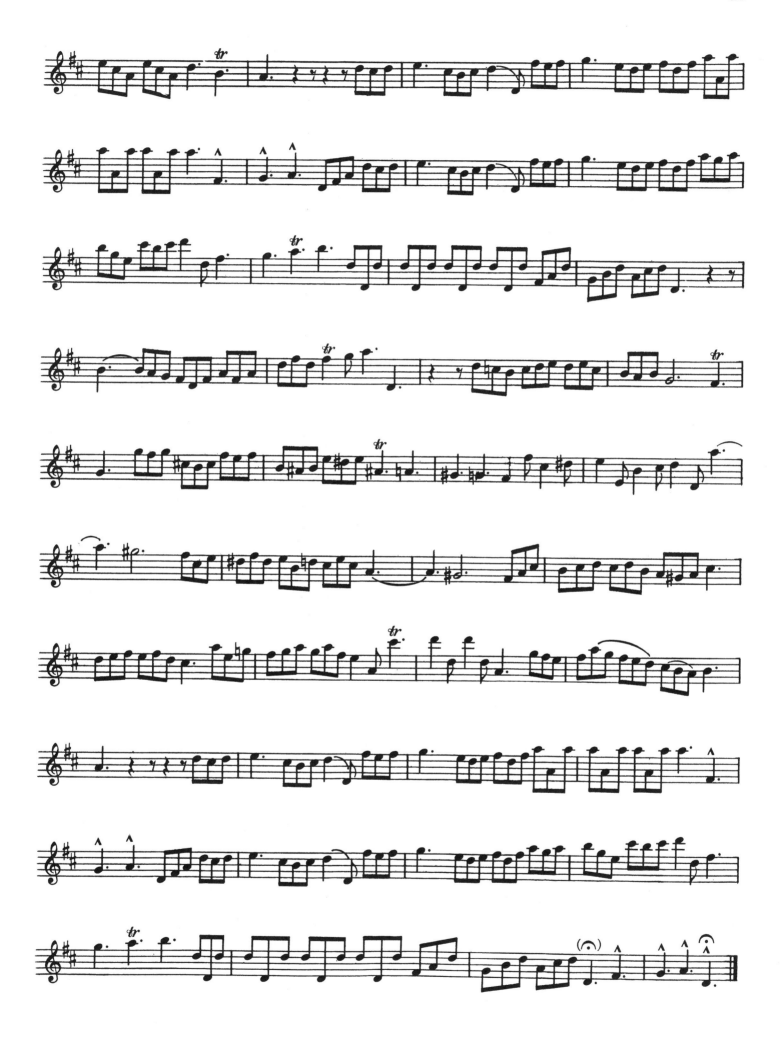

FROM DUETTO No. IV

W. F. BACH

* When ♪. ♪ is played against a triplet, play it ♪ ♪

GEMINIANI

SONATA No. V

*HANDEL

Largo [in eight]

* Probably composed by G.C. Schultze.

SONATA No. 3

DEVIENNE

RONDEAU
Allegro vivace

Two Duets
Selected from the Sonatas of J. B. Loeillet

ADAGIO AND ALLEGRO FROM SONATA No. 1

J. B. LOEILLET

Allegro

SONATA No. III

J. B. LOEILLET

Giga [Allegro]

Duetto No. I
Based on Sonata in Bb, K. 378

MOZART

Andante sostenuto

RONDO
Allegro molto

Allegro assai

Duetto No. II
Based on Sonata in F, K. 376

MOZART

RONDO
Allegretto grazioso

69